Megan Gets a Dollhouse

by NANCY McARTHUR

illustrated by MEGAN LLOYD

SCHOLASTIC INC.

New York   Toronto   London   Auckland   Sydney

To Russell, Irene, Susan, and John McArthur
with special thanks to Barbara Barstow, Marjorie Shannon Bryant,
and Rachel and Jennifer Reichert
—N. Mc.

For Squeak and Taffy
—M.L.

ISBN 0-590-40831-3

Text copyright © 1988 by Nancy McArthur.
Illustrations copyright © 1988 by Megan Lloyd.
All rights reserved. Published by Scholastic Inc.

HELLO, READER is a trademark of Scholastic Inc.
Art direction by Diana Hrisinko
Book design by Theresa Fitzgerald

12 11 10 9 8 7 6 5 4 3 2   8 9/8 0 1 2 3/9

Printed in the U.S.A.   08
First Scholastic printing, January 1988

Megan's cousin Sharon had a beautiful dollhouse.

Everything in it was perfect. It even had little fake food in the kitchen.

Megan wanted to move the furniture around.

"Don't move that!" Sharon said every time. "That's right where I want it."

So Megan just picked things up and looked at them.

"Be careful," Sharon kept saying. "Don't break that."

Megan wished her cat Fluffo could come over to Sharon's house. Fluffo loved to squash himself into small places like drawers and paper bags and just sit there.

If he were here, Fluffo could squash himself into Sharon's dollhouse and knock everything over. Thinking about that made Megan laugh out loud.

"What are you laughing about?" asked Sharon.

"I'm thinking about Fluffo."

"What a dumb name for a cat," said Sharon.

"My brother named him that," said Megan, "because he feels soft and fluffy."

Megan wanted a dollhouse of her own. Then
she could move everything around every day.
    Maybe sometimes she would take the
furniture out of one room. She would let Fluffo
squash himself in and just sit there.
    He would love that.

"I really want a dollhouse," she told Mom.
"They cost a lot," said Mom. "We'll see."
They went to a dollhouse store.

"These are perfect," said Mom, "but they all
cost a fortune. Maybe Dad could build one."
"Does Dad know how to build things?"
asked Megan.
"Maybe he could learn," said Mom.

"Could you make me a dollhouse?" Megan asked Dad.

"I could figure out how," he said. "You and Mike could help. We'll make lots of rooms and a stairway. That would be perfect."

"Can we buy some wood and start right now?" asked Megan.

"No, first I have to borrow or rent some power tools. Then I have to learn to saw and drill holes with them."

"Then can we start?"

"No, first I'd better build something easy, like a bird feeder."

Dad looked out the window as if he could already see the feeder out there.

"We'll buy a bird book," he said. "You and Mike can learn all about birds."

"What about my dollhouse?" asked Megan.

"It will take me a while to learn to make something that hard," he replied.

Mom said, "Maybe we could find a kit that just glues together."

"No," said Dad. "If I'm going to do it, I'm going to do it right. It will be perfect. Just like a real house."

He started out the back door. "I'm going to see where to put the bird feeder."

Megan thought it would be a long time before she got her dollhouse.

She plopped down on the kitchen floor next to a cardboard box from the grocery store.

One side had a little hole in it.
Megan peeked in.
It was like looking through a little window into a little house.
Suddenly, looking back at her from the little window, was...

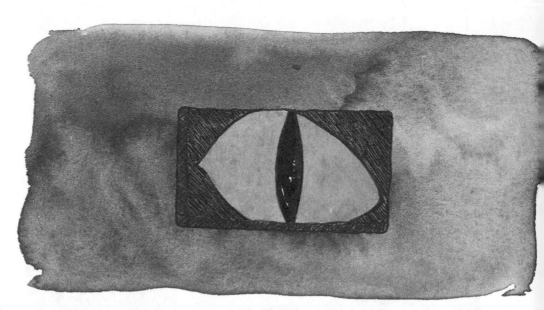

...a big yellow eye.

Fluffo's big furry paw came out and tapped her on the nose.

"This would be a good little dollhouse," she told Fluffo.

With a pencil Megan drew a door and more windows.

Mom would not let her use a sharp knife, so she got her brother Mike to help. He cut only three sides of the door, so it bent to open and close.

They looked through the door and windows.

"This is neat," said Mike. "You should paint the walls green."

"I don't want green," said Megan.

She liked green, but she did not want Mike to tell her what to do.

She walked two fingers through the door and into the house. She said in a high squeaky voice, "What a nice little house! I think I'll live here."

Megan used her poster paint to paint one wall red.

"Red is not a wall color," said Mike.

"I like red," said Megan.

That color was almost gone, so she painted the second wall yellow.

"Walls are supposed to be the same," said Mike.

"I want different colors," said Megan.

She painted the third wall purple.

"That looks good," she said.

Megan wondered what color to make the fourth wall.

"How about wallpaper?" asked Mom. "You could paste on some gift wrap paper."

Megan found some left over from her birthday. It was green with pink teddy bears all over it. She cut a big piece and put it on the wall.

"You pasted it over the window," said Mike.

"This wall doesn't need a window," Megan said.

She waited until he went away. Then she poked a hole in the paper to make the window again.

Megan found a piece of wood to be a bed and another to be a table.

She used a little piece of cloth for a bedspread.

She found a big bottle top to be a wastebasket.

She tore bits off a paper napkin and squashed them to put in her wastebasket.

She cut a birthday candle in half to make two little ones.

She found some big buttons that looked like plates.

Everywhere Megan looked she found things that could be something else.

"Where's the toothpaste top?" yelled Dad.

It was in Megan's dollhouse being a lamp shade.

"Where's my nail polish?" called Mom.

Megan was using it to paint her table pink.

"Where's the other place mat?" shouted Mike as he set the table.

It was in Megan's dollhouse being a rug.

She cut little pictures out of magazines to paste on the wall. Dad helped her make curtains.

Megan put bits of hamburger on her table. That was better than the fake food in Sharon's house.

But Fluffo ate it.

So she crunched up some corn flakes very small to put in her bottle cap bowls.

Fluffo did not like corn flakes.

Megan's house was one big room with parts of all kinds of rooms in it.

"You can't have a bed in the kitchen," said Mike.

"I want it there," said Megan. "That's for if you get tired waiting for food to cook, then you can take a nap."

Megan kept the top of the box closed, but
Fluffo knew how to get it open.
He loved to sneak in and just sit there.

When Megan played in the house, Fluffo
scrunched down outside it and played King
Kong.
She saw a big yellow eye looking in the
window.
Then a big furry paw came in and...

WHACK! Things went flying.
   Megan was glad to see her furniture did
not break.

Sharon's house was too big and perfect to
move around, but Megan could carry hers
anywhere she wanted.

At night she put it next to her bed.

She walked two fingers in and said squeakily,
"Good-night, everybody. Time to go to sleep."

She closed her eyes and pretended she was sleeping in the little wooden bed with the cotton puff pillow.

She felt Fluffo snuggle up next to her.

Maybe he was dreaming that he was alseep on the little bed, too.

Megan took her house along in the car to go to Grandma's.

"I like your teddy bear wallpaper," said Grandma.

She let Megan look through her wastebaskets for little things that could be something for her dollhouse.

She found some plastic pieces that could be chairs, and bottle caps for pie pans.

"You have good trash," said Megan.

Then they made cookies.

Grandma also put some tiny drops of dough on the pan.

"These will be baby cookies for your house," she said.

Megan kept the special cookies in her house a whole day. Then she ate them all.

When Megan took her house out to play in the backyard, she would not let Fluffo come out, too.

Her friend Rachael came over.

Megan walked her fingers around in the house and said, "Come in and visit."

Rachael walked her fingers in. "This is nice," she said. "Can I stay for dinner?"

"Yes," squeaked Megan. "Have some corn flakes."

Fluffo sat in the sunny kitchen window watching them.

Megan hurried to get her dollhouse ready to show off.

Sharon was coming over.

To keep Fluffo out, Megan put the house up on a table.

There was not enough room on the edge for a big cat.

But nothing stopped Fluffo.

He made a giant leap.

His whole head went into a window and
got stuck.

His back legs started sliding off the table.

The house was waving around on his head.

Everything inside was crashing around.

Megan grabbed Fluffo with one hand. She held the house down with the other.

Now she was stuck, too.

She could not let go of either one without a very big crash.

"Help!" she yelled.

Mike came running. He grabbed Fluffo, and Megan got the house off his head.

She held Fluffo for a while to make him feel better.

Then she started all over to get the house ready.

She got done just in time.

Sharon walked around the little house.

"This is cute," she said. "What kind of furniture do you have?"

"Look in the window," said Megan. "That's fun."

Sharon got down on the floor and peeked in.

A big furry paw bopped her right on the nose.
"EEEEEK!" screeched Sharon.
"Don't worry," said Megan. "It's only Fluffo
Kong."
She pulled Fluffo out of the house and put
things back in place again.

"This bed would look better over there," said Sharon.

"Don't move that," said Megan. "It's right where I want it."

Then she said, "But you can pick things up. My stuff doesn't break."

They had a good time playing with Megan's dollhouse.

After Sharon went home, Megan looked
for Fluffo.

She wanted to hold him and scratch behind
his ears. He loved that.

She knew where to find him.
Her house was purring.
She opened the top.

Fluffo jumped out onto her lap and purred.